There were five in the bed.

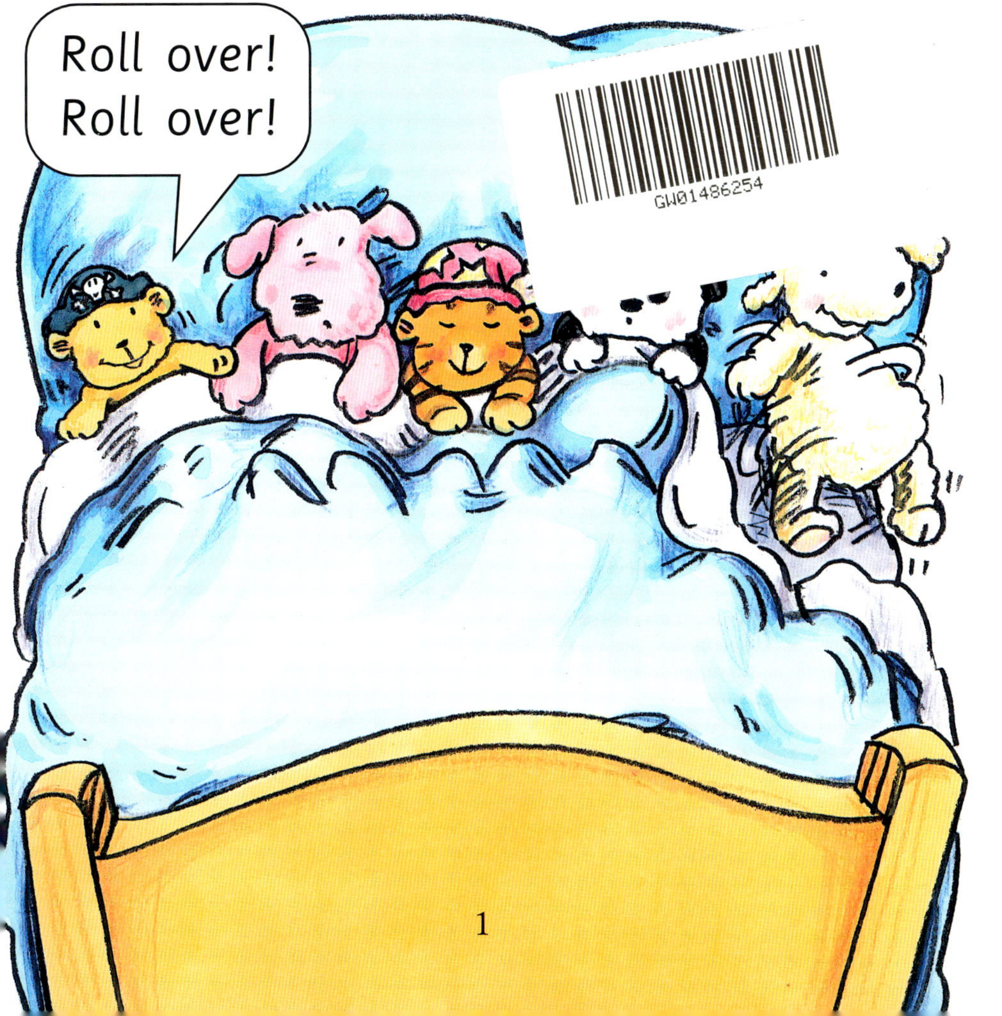
Roll over!
Roll over!

There were

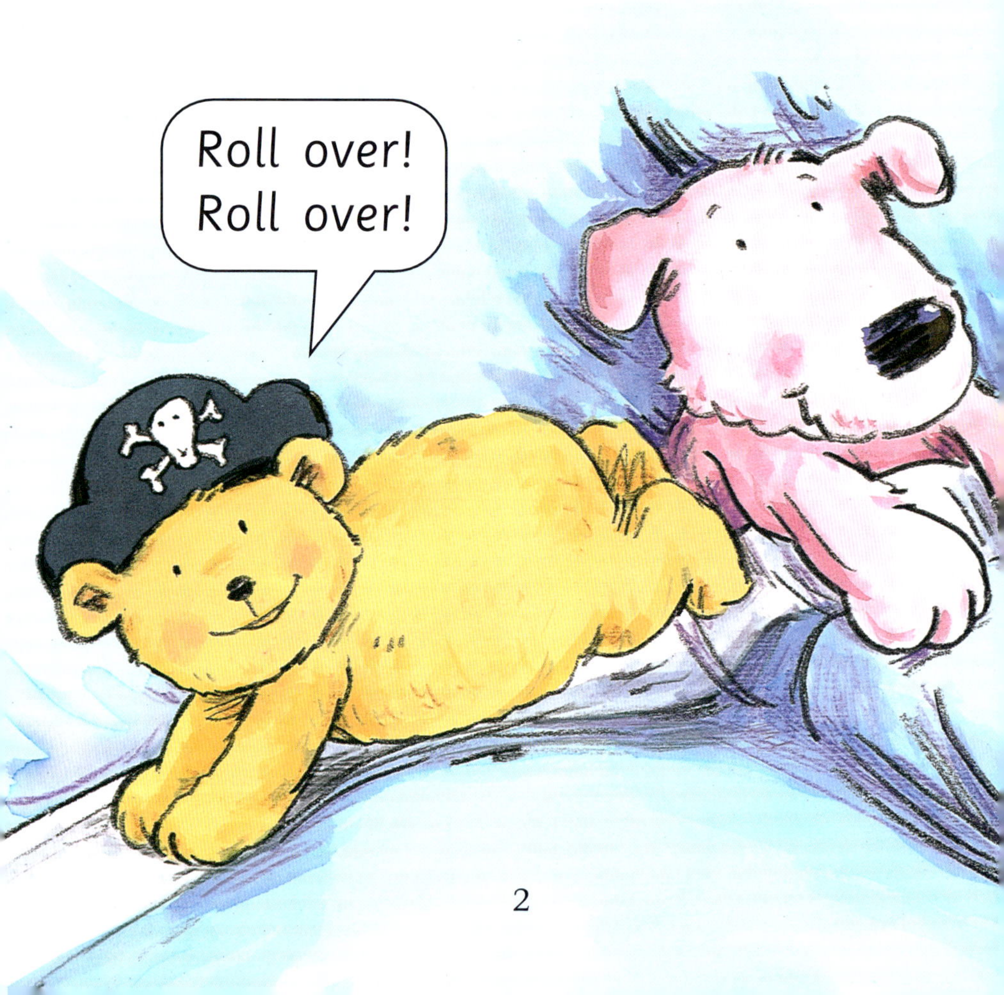
Roll over!
Roll over!

four in the bed.

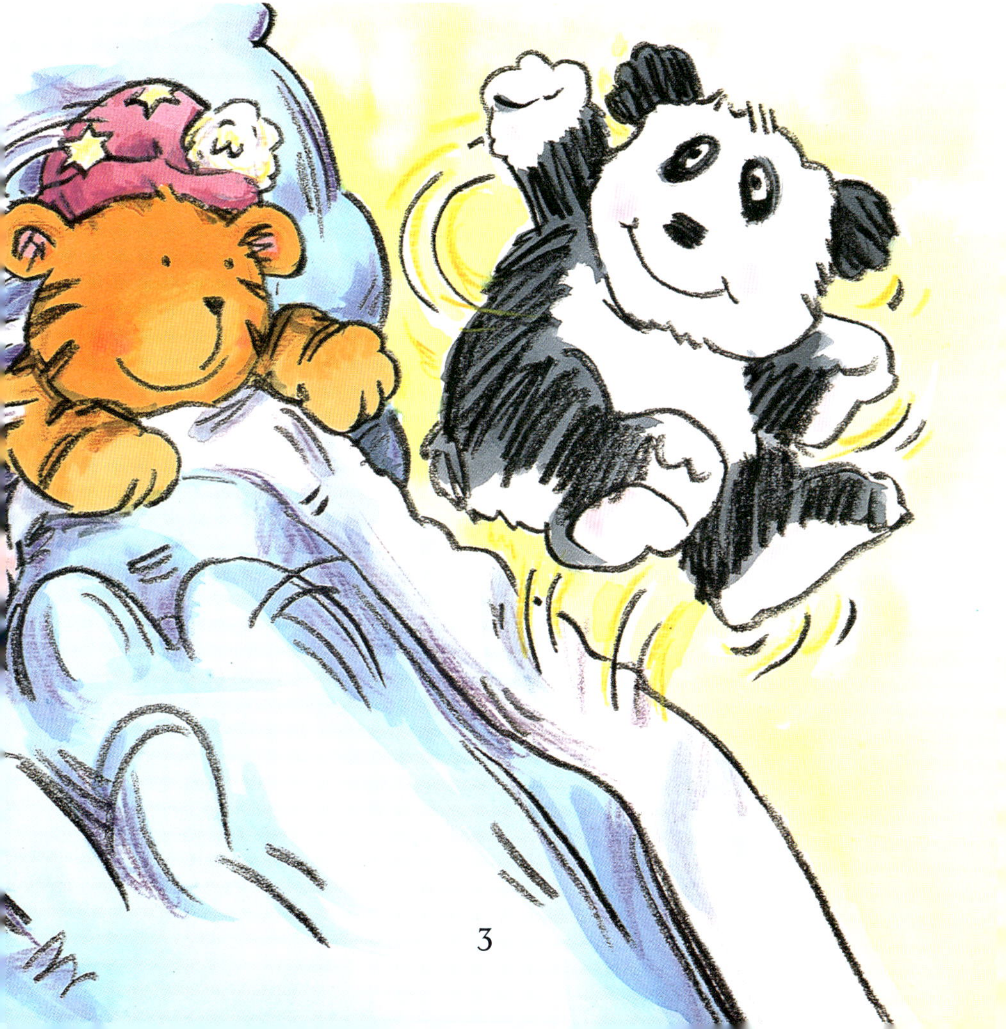

There were

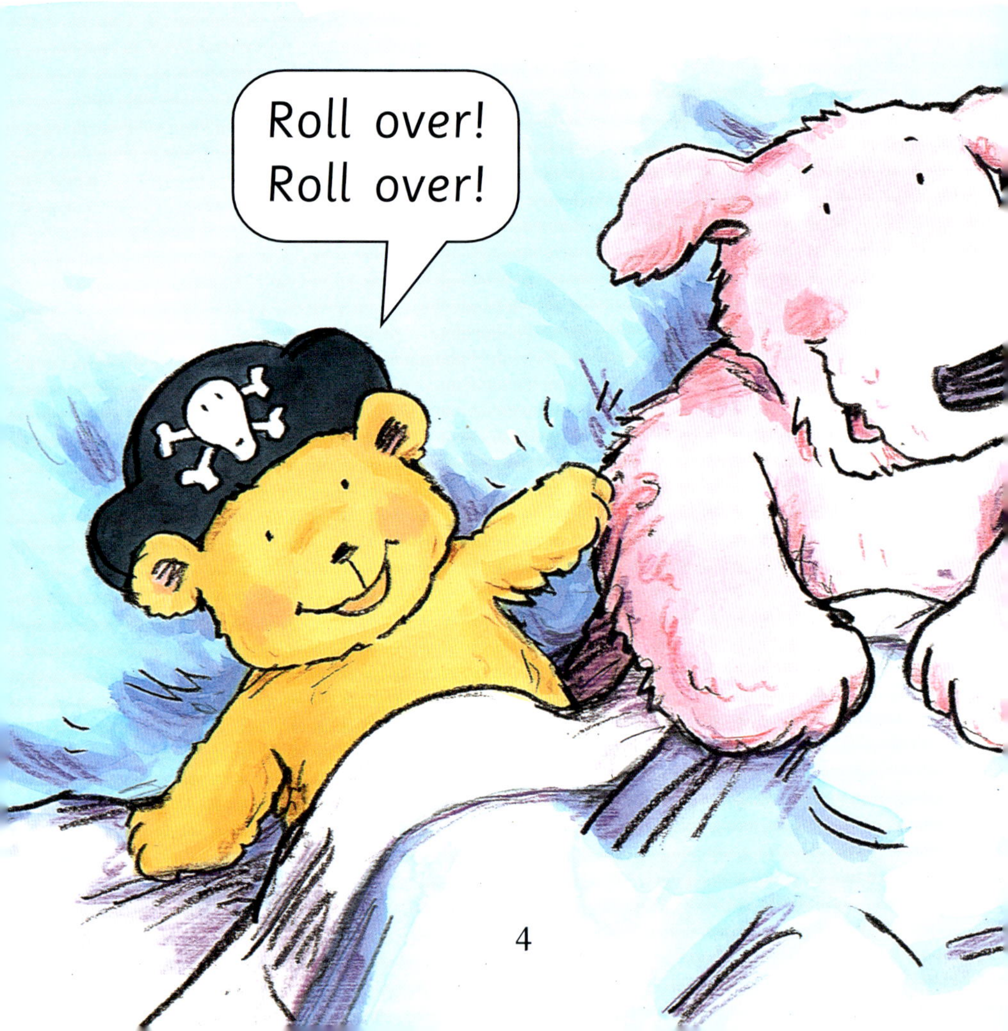

three in the bed.

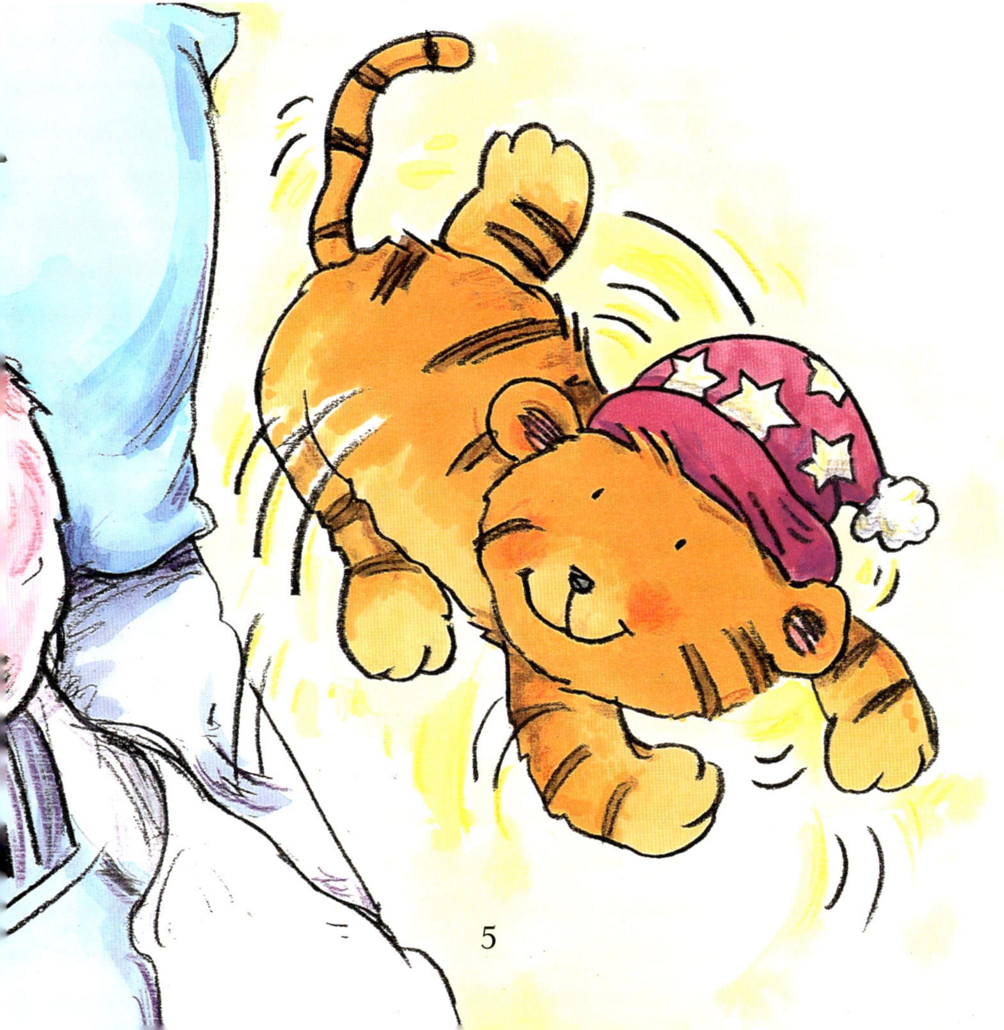

There were

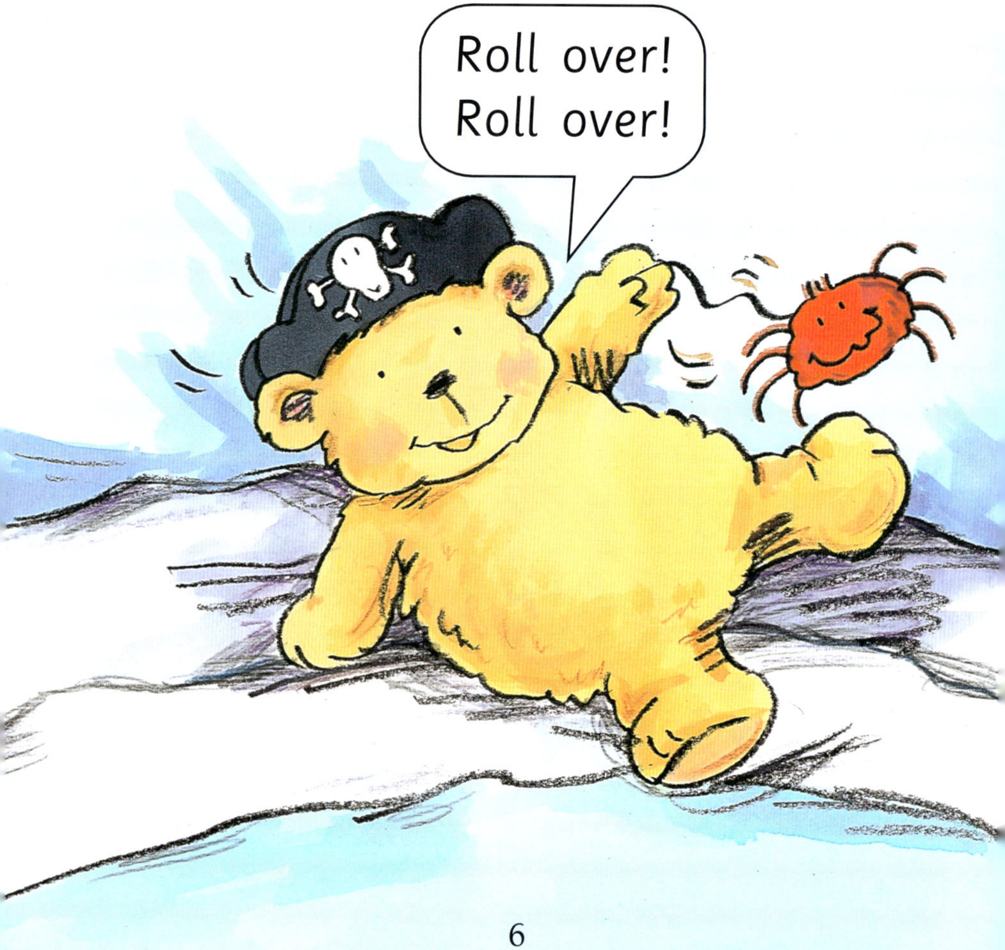

two in the bed.

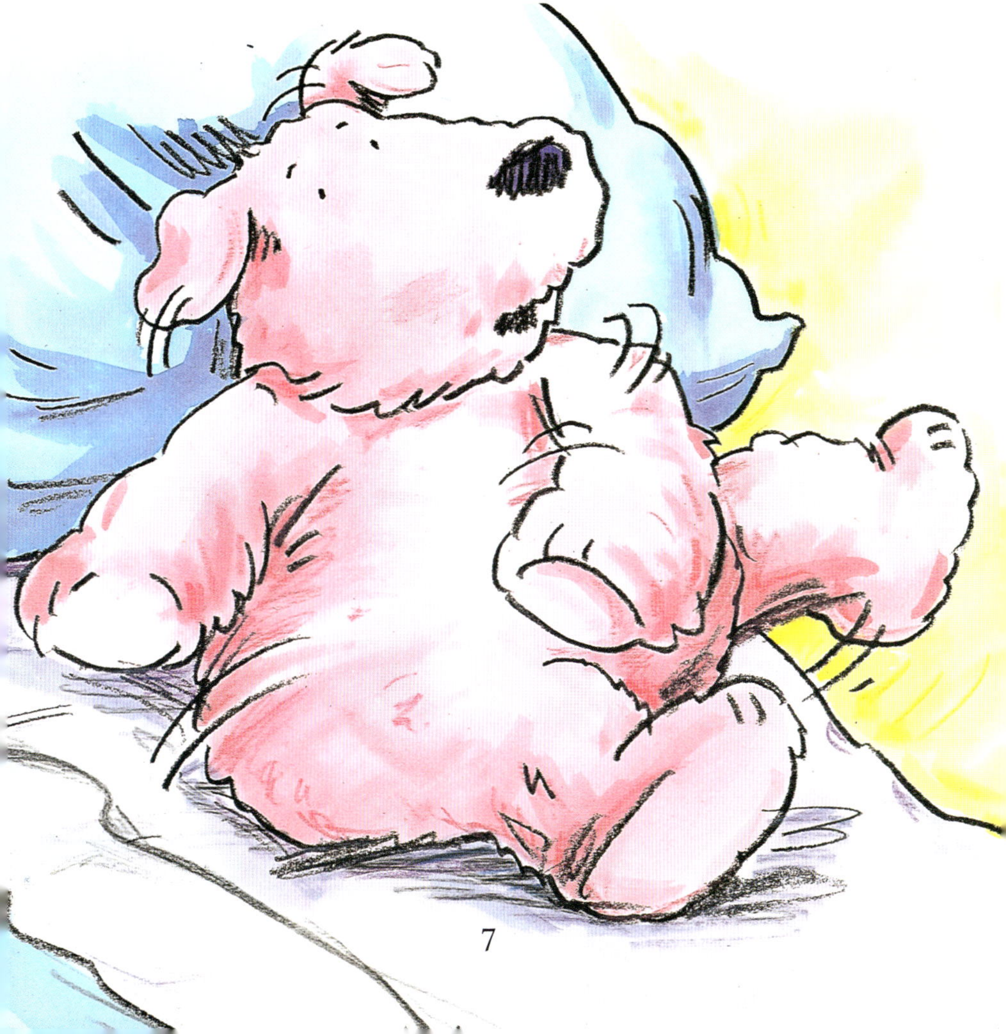

There was one in the bed.

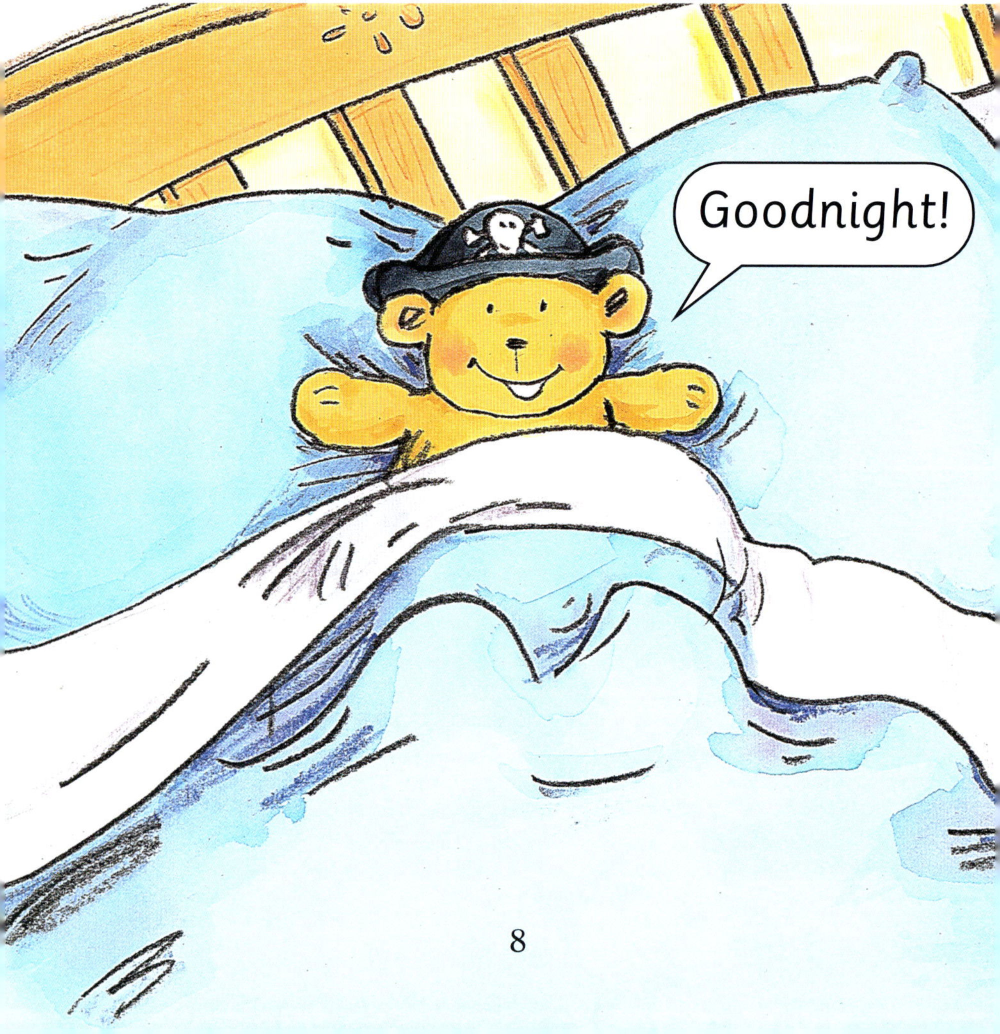